Knowing Who You Are In Christ

Deloris R. Brown

Copyright © 2019 Deloris R. Brown

All rights reserved.

ISBN: 9781690849582

DEDICATION:

This book is dedicated to my parents, Rev. Garfield & Lillie Mae Richardson, both who are now deceased, who taught me values in life that I now continue to live by. Also, I want to dedicate this book to my husband, Larry of many years, that has given me the chance to travel to many destinations with him in his Military career. He has also helped me to grow spiritually by his Godly example. To my dear son, Stephen that has given me joy and inspiration since the day he was born.

A very special thank you to Pastor Paul DeNeui, who was very instrumental in helping me understand the process and procedures necessary in getting this book published. He was most helpful! And again, my heartfelt thanks go to him.

Most of all, I am truly thankful and grateful to God for placing it in my heart, the urge to inform my Christian brothers and sisters of Who We Are In Christ. We should never take for granted what we are afforded: awesome positions, privileges and responsibilities because of Him- Jesus Christ!

FOREWORD:

We are aware of the situations going on all around us with all the radical groups and all of the things they are doing trying to instill fear within the hearts of many, but Psalm 27:1-3 declares, "The Lord is my light and my salvation; whom shall I fear? The Lord is the strength of my life; of whom shall I be afraid?

Vs. 2 – When the wicked, even mine enemies and my foes, came upon me to eat up my flesh, they stumbled and fell.

Vs. 3 – Though an host should encamp against me, my heart shall not fear: though war should rise against me, in this will I be confident."

We hear of wars and rumors of wars as Jesus tells us about in the gospel of Matthew chapter 24. So we don't need to let our hearts be troubled, but as the Body of Christ, we need to arise and take our rightful place while we are still here on the earth. We need to understand that according to the word of God, that in the end – as the Body of Christ – WE WIN! We have read the back of the book (the bible,) and it let's us know that 'WE WIN.'

Before the return of Jesus, we have to get in our place as His Body and know 'Who We Are,' and what His plan and purpose is

Knowing Who You Are In Christ

for our life.

This book is born out of my desire to see the church – Jesus' bride, know exactly who they are and fulfill His commission while here in the earth. His commission is still the same as when He gave that commission to His disciples – "Go ye therefore, and teach all nations, baptizing them in the name of the Father, and of the Son, and of the Holy Ghost."

Radical groups are killing people that don't think like they think, or in actuality, they are being perpetrated and used by the devil. This should be nothing new for the child of God, because Jesus said, "since the days of John the Baptist, the earth has suffered violence, but the violent taketh by force." So as children of the most High God, we have spiritual weapons we need to use now as never before. It is my desire that for some of you, it will be a reminder of these weapons, and they are here for us to use each and everyday, and for others coming into the knowledge of who you are in Christ will give you the desire to hunger for more of the knowledge of what belongs to you as a child of God.

<u>Knowing Who you Are in Christ</u> gives you the assurance that "A thousand shall fall at thy side, and ten thousand at thy right hand; but it shall not come nigh thee."(<u>Psalm 91:7</u>) We have nothing to fear!

Deloris R. Brown

As children of God, we have been given rights and privileges. We have been blessed with manifold blessings and benefits that the world cannot even begin to fathom. <u>Ephesians 1: 3</u> – "Blessed be the God and Father of our Lord Jesus Christ, who <u>hath</u> (past tense) blessed us with all spiritual blessings in heavenly places in Christ:"

Now is the time for the Body of Christ to arise, take your place and let the world know that according to <u>Ephesians 3:10</u> -" To the intent that now unto the principalities and powers in heavenly places might be known by the church the manifold wisdom of God."

Knowing Who You Are In Christ

CONTENTS

	Acknowledgments	i
1	KNOWING WHO YOU ARE IN CHRIST – YOU KNOW THAT YOUR SINS HAVE BEEN FORGIVEN!	1
2	KNOWING WHO YOU ARE IN CHRIST GIVES YOU THE ASSURANCE THAT YOU ARE BLESSED!	7
3	BECAUSE YOU KNOW WHO YOU ARE IN CHRIST, YOU'VE BEEN BLESSED TO BE A BLESSING	14
4	HEALING BELONGS TO YOU BECAUSE OF WHO YOU ARE IN CHRIST	17
5	ANGELS HAVE BEEN ASSIGNED TO YOU!	22
6	YOU HAVE BEEN GIVEN AUTHORITY	26
7	HOLINESS IS STILL REQUIRED	32
8	WE HAVE THE ASSURANCE THAT HEAVEN WILL BE OUR FINAL & ETERNAL DESTINATION	38
	CONCLUSION	42

CHAPTER 1

KNOWING WHO YOU ARE IN CHRIST –YOU KNOW THAT YOUR SINS HAVE BEEN FORGIVEN

As born again believers, we believe that we are coming to the close of this age - the age of Grace. We have to know who we are in Christ; all He has done for us and all He will continue to do until we are taken out of here. First and foremost, Jesus paid a tremendous price for us to be able to choose and accept Him as our personal Savior. He made us a new creature – a species that never existed before.

2 Corinthians 5:17 –"Therefore if any man be in Christ, he is a

new creature: old things are passed away; behold, all things are become new." 2 Corinthians 5:17 in the Amplified Bible says – "Therefore if any person is (ingrafted) in Christ, the Messiah, he is (a new creature altogether,) a new creation; the old (previous moral and spiritual condition) has passed away. Behold, the fresh and new has come!" In other words, your spirit man has become new – the real you! You are a spirit, you have a soul (your mind, your will and your emotions;) and you have a body. Your body looked the same when you got saved or born again; the work was done on the inside when you received the Spirit of God. You have to renew your mind with the word of God. Your body will line up with the word of God as you renew your mind with the word of God.

Romans 12:1-2:

"I Beseech you therefore, brethren, by the mercies of God, that ye present your bodies a living sacrifice, holy, acceptable unto God, which is your reasonable service.

Vs. 2 – And be not conformed to this world: but be ye transformed by the renewing of your mind, that ye may prove what is that good, and acceptable, and perfect, will of God."

So when you get born again, your body will still want to do what it's use to doing. For example, if going to the club and partying was what you liked to do, your flesh or body will still want to do that, but you have got to get into the word of God, and as you continue to read, study and grow in the word of God and fellowship with brothers and sisters, your body will line up and not want to do contrary things to the Word of God. So many times before this process takes place, we will see people give up and go back to living the same life they lived before they were born again. They will tell you that they just can't live like that. Why? It is because they didn't continue in the word of God. We often come in contact with people that are saved or born again, but have not renewed their mind with the Word of God. We see them in the same state they were in when they first came to the Lord and the church - not growing in the things of God at all; we call this remaining a 'babe in Christ.' They refuse, or are ignorant (not knowing) that there's a process that they have to go through in becoming all that God wants them to become. When going through a process, it takes time. When coming out of the world, it takes time to conform or change into what God wants for your life. This is where the mature saints will have to be patient with the 'babes' in Christ. We have to give them time to grow. That's why He tells us to be transformed by the renewing of the mind. Being a 'babe' in Christ, is not where you want to remain, but you want to grow up in Christ and take your place in the Body of Christ. This is God's plan and purpose for you!

Forget your past! It doesn't exist anymore. I'm talking about your past mistakes; your past failures. This is something that you need to accept. You have to believe 2 Corinthians 5:17 – "Therefore if any man be in Christ, he is a new creature: old things are passed away; behold, all things are become new." When you were born again, you became a new creation. As long as you keep looking back at your past, you can't move forward in the things of God. When the devil comes into your mind and begin to play games with you about your past, or he uses someone to try to remind you of your past - stop him in his tracks. Begin by speaking out of your mouth – you don't fight thoughts with thoughts, but you have to speak the word of God out of your mouth. Tell the devil, you are right, that was me, but Jesus made me new; a new creation that has never existed before. Stop him or he will have you remember when……………………!!! Oh, no, stop him quickly and begin to do what Philippians 4:8 says to do:

Philippians 4:8 says, - "Finally, brethren, whatsoever things are true, whatsoever things are honest, whatsoever things are just, whatsoever things are pure, whatsoever things are lovely, whatsoever things are of good report; if there be any virtue, and if there be any praise, think on these things." Tell the devil, "don't bring up my past, because I don't have one." He only brings up your past because he's intimidated by your present. I said he's intimidated by your present. He knows that God has some awesome things for your life if you just don't quit! You need to know that you can begin again and again and again. Thank God!

So be about your Father's business and forget your past – you can't move forward as long as you are staring back at your past. Begin to move forward and watch God as He does some awesome things in you and through you. Remember, your mess truly can become your message, and God can get the glory out of your life. Isaiah 1:18 says, - "Come now, and let us reason together, saith the Lord: though your sins be as scarlet, they shall be as white as snow; though they be red like crimson, they shall be as wool."

Psalm 103:12 says, -"As far as the east is from the west, so far hath he removed our transgressions from us." Thank God we are free from our past sins and mistakes, and don't let anyone condemn you because of your past. Jesus' shed blood have taken care of the sin problem in our lives and the sins of the whole world. So, you be free in Jesus Name! Just as He admonished us in the book of Isaiah "to come reason together," He has given us the New Testament which is a better covenant with better promises – Hebrews 8:6 says, – "But now hath He obtained a more excellent ministry, by how much also He is the mediator of a better covenant, which was established upon better promises."

Always remember that as long as you keep looking back at your past, you can't move forward into the destiny God has for you! Take your rightful place and let God be glorified in and through your life…

I'm reminded of the woman with the alabaster box that washed Jesus feet with her tears, and wiped them with the hairs of her head: He said of her in Luke 7:47-48 – "Wherefore I say unto thee, Her sins, which are many, are forgiven; for she loved much: but to whom little is forgiven, the same loveth little.

Vs. 48 – And He said unto her, Thy sins are forgiven."

Remember: Your Sins Are Forgiven!

CHAPTER 2

KNOWING WHO YOU ARE IN CHRIST GIVES YOU THE ASSURANCE THAT YOU ARE BLESSED

As children of Almighty God, it is His will to bless us! Ephesians 1:3 says, -"Blessed be the God and Father of our Lord Jesus Christ, who hath blessed us with all spiritual blessings in heavenly places in Christ:" This is past tense- hath blessed. This means that everything we need have already been provided for us by God. He has done all He is going to do. We have to position ourselves and appropriate what has already been given to us by God. You may ask, well, you say everything has been given to us, how do I obtain all of this? You have to use your faith. We have all been given the measure of faith according to Romans 12:3 – "For I say, through the grace given unto me, to every man that is among you, not to think of himself more highly than he ought to think; but to think soberly, according as God hath dealt to every man the measure of faith."

Hebrews 11:6 – "But without faith it is impossible to please Him: for he that cometh to God must believe that He is, and that He is a rewarder of them that diligently seek Him." We obtain these blessings by faith in God. I don't see it, but I trust (lean and rely) on you God to bring it to pass. This is where your patience and determination plays an important part. You position yourself (by being faithful and committed to God) until what you are believing God for is manifested or brought into the natural realm. Sometimes, you are on the very brink of a miracle or the manifestation of what you are believing God for, and just when God gets ready to meet your need, you give up and quit believing. You quit exercising your faith too soon. No, hang in there until you see the manifestation of your miracle. God wants you blessed! You have to learn to endure hardness as a good soldier as Apostle Paul told Timothy in:

2 Timothy 2:3 – "Thou therefore endure hardness, as a good soldier of Jesus Christ." In the age in which we live now, nobody wants to endure. I want it now, fast and in a hurry- microwave it if necessary! Some things you have to learn to wait on. You have to endure some things! You have to get to the point where you say to God, "God, I've been waiting for awhile now,

but I don't mind waiting on you. I will continue to wait, because I know that when the manifestation takes place, it will be at the right and appointed time. Furthermore God, I will be of good courage while I wait." Psalm 27:14 says, —" Wait on the Lord: be of good courage, and He shall strengthen thine heart: wait, I say, on the Lord." God knows what we need and when we need it. Most of the time, we may be in a hurry, but we must remember, He is in no hurry —He is not on a time schedule. God doesn't get in a hurry, but He meets us just when the timing is right! He always comes to our rescue; what an awesome God we serve!

You need to know and understand that God doesn't bless us to hoard it up for ourselves, but He blesses us to be a blessing. I've heard people say things like, "I don't want to be rich, but I want just enough to get by — me, my four, and no more!" I want to tell them so badly, "dear heart, you are trying to sound humble, but that is not scriptural." The Word of God says, "Let the Lord be magnified, which hath pleasure in the prosperity of His servant." Psalm 35:27b and Proverbs 10:22 says, — "The blessing of the Lord, it maketh rich, and He addeth no sorrow with it." Psalm 112:1-3 says — "Praise ye the Lord. Blessed is the man that feareth the Lord, that delighteth greatly in His commandments.

Vs. 2 - His seed shall be mighty upon earth: the generation of the upright shall be blessed.

Vs 3 – Wealth and riches shall be in his house: and his righteousness endureth for ever."

3 John 2 says, – "Beloved, I wish above all things that thou mayest prosper and be in health, even as thy soul prospereth." So, God doesn't mind you having things, but He doesn't want things to have you to the point that you can't give Him the glory for what He blesses you with. Always be willing to accept all that God has for you with a grateful heart. If He blesses you to the point that you don't need it, by all means, be willing to be a blessing to others – in other words, give it away! Always remember that if God can get it through you, He can get it to you. Be willing to share your blessings with the many Missionaries on foreign soil proclaiming the gospel (good news) of Jesus Christ. Be willing to share with someone that may not have clean drinking water; share with Bible Schools that are preparing and propelling men and women forth to take the glorious gospel into places you and I may never be able to go; sow into other ministries that God may lay on your heart. Make no mistake about it, God doesn't mind His children having abundance, but what He is concerned about is money not having them. Let's look at an example in the bible where we find a young man that has abundance and if you notice, abundance has him. Let's look at Luke18:18-23 – "And a certain

ruler asked Him, saying, Good Master, what shall I do to inherit eternal life?

Vs 19 – And Jesus said unto him, Why callest thou me good? none is good, save one, that is, God.

Vs 20 – Thou knowest the commandments, Do not commit adultery, Do not kill, Do not steal, Do not bear false witness, Honor thy father and thy mother.

Vs 21 – And he said, All these have I kept from my youth up.

Vs 22 – Now when Jesus heard these things, He said unto him, Yet lackest thou one thing: sell all that thou hast, and distribute unto the poor, and thou shalt have treasure in heaven: and come, follow me.

Vs 23 – And when he heard this, he was very sorrowful: for he was very rich." This young man thought he had it going on – until he met Jesus face to face. He simply lacked one thing – he wouldn't let go of his riches. Luke 18:23 – "And when he heard this, he was very sorrowful;" for he was not just rich – Jesus said he was "very rich."

Jesus knew that even though this rich young ruler had all the right words, Jesus also knew his heart. You see, the bible tells us that man looks at the outward appearance, but Jesus looks at the heart. He knows your heart – you may be saying the right things, but what is your heart really saying? I believe that Jesus would have given him more than he had if he had just followed Jesus. There are not many places in the Bible where Jesus tells someone to come follow Him. He chose His twelve disciples and told them to come follow Him, but many times when He healed someone and they wanted to follow Him, He would tell them to go home and tell what great things was done. We also see in Luke 12:16-21 – "And He spake a parable unto them, saying, The ground of a certain rich man brought forth plentifully:

Vs 17 - And he thought within himself, saying, What shall I do, because I have no room where to bestow my fruits?

Vs 18 – And he said, This will I do: I will pull down my barns and build greater; and there will I bestow all my fruits and my goods.

Vs 19 – And I will say to my soul, Soul, thou hast much goods laid up for many years; take thine ease, eat, drink, and be merry.

Vs 20 – But God said unto him, Thou fool, this night thy soul shall be required of thee: then whose shall those things be, which thou hast provided?

Vs 21 – So is he that layeth up treasure for himself, and is not rich toward God."

Knowing Who You Are In Christ

This is another account of someone trying to hold on to things just for himself. But the bible says in Matthew 6:33 – "But seek ye first the kingdom of God, and His righteousness; and all these things shall be added unto you."

Sometimes we try hard to hold on to what little we have instead of letting go, and let God do the addition and multiplication – oh, by the way, He is a great mathematician. He operates in addition and multiplication while the devil operates in subtraction and division.

God truly wants to bless His children to the point where there will never be lack or want in a household. Learn to trust Him completely!

Money is not the only thing He wants to bless you with. He wants to bless you with health; long life and He wants your family blessed and He wants your joy to be full!

Hebrews 11:6 – "But without faith it is impossible to please Him: for he that cometh to God must believe that He is, and that He is a rewarder of them that diligently seek Him."

CHAPTER 3

BECAUSE YOU KNOW WHO YOU ARE IN CHRIST, YOU'VE BEEN BLESSED TO BE A BLESSING

Luke 6:38 says, – "Give, and it shall be given unto you; good measure, pressed down, and shaken together, and running over, shall men give into your bosom. For with the same measure that ye mete withal it shall be measured to you again."

In the thirty eight(38) years that I have been born again, this scripture has been one of my favorites. Jesus was speaking and He said if you give, I tell you what will happen – it is going to be given back to you - good measure, pressed down and shaken together, and running over, shall men give to you. What a breakthrough this could bring into your life if you really understood this scripture. You see, Jesus doesn't need anything from us except our willingness and obedience to serve Him – yet He gives us the privilege to secure financial wealth, healing from sickness and disease and anything else that your heart desires just by simply giving. Yet you have many people that have a problem with tithing or giving into the Kingdom of God simply because they do not understand the benefits that they reap when they open their heart and give back to God. You give most of all because you love God!

Each morning, wake up and ask the Lord, "who can I be a blessing too on today?" Money doesn't always have to be involved – it can, but doesn't have to be. Give a smile to someone; help a mother struggling with a stroller and trying to open a door; give a kind word when the Holy Spirit prompts you too. Sometimes a kind word will do wonders to lift a weary spirit. The list goes on, but determine that as a child of God, you will be a blessing everywhere you go, and if you purpose to listen, God will instruct you; we are to be imitators of Jesus Christ! Jesus wants to be personified in you!

Galatians 6:9 says – "And let us not be weary in well doing: for in due season we shall reap, if we faint not." We have so many precious promises from God!

On our recent Women's Retreat in the beautiful mountains of

Deloris R. Brown

Asheville, North Carolina, I had the opportunity to witness the power of what effect a kind word and the willingness to pray had on someone; I had the opportunity to observe one of the Ministers in the group willing to pray for a stranger we met; as a matter of fact, she prayed for several people on this Retreat. One particular older gentleman had a cast on his arm. What touched my heart was as she approached him and asked if he would permit her to pray, he gladly accepted the offer and also told the Minister that he was having a problem with his eyes. Blindness was trying to set in and as she prayed for him, he was so grateful. Kindness is contagious! Always remember that we are Jesus' representatives here in the earth.

Know that you were created in God's likeness and His image, and if Jesus were in the earth today, He would truly make a lasting impression everywhere He would go. What about you, my friend? Are you leaving an impression everywhere you go? Purpose to be a blessing everywhere you go! Remember, you are fearfully and wonderfully made. Psalm 139:14 says – "I will praise thee; for I am fearfully and wonderfully made: marvelous are thy works; and that my soul knoweth right well." Our hearts desire should be to be imitators of Christ everywhere we go, knowing that we are blessed to be a blessing!

CHAPTER 4

HEALING BELONGS TO YOU BECAUSE OF WHO YOU ARE IN CHRIST

In the body of Christ, sickness seems to be an everyday occurrence –the new norm is what they call it! Sickness runs rampant just as it does in the world, but according to the word of God, healing belongs to us. When you try to explain to some people that healing is for today, some will use the cliché "I just call it what it is." I believe Isaiah 53: 5 says -"But He was wounded for our transgressions, He was bruised for our iniquities: the chastisement of our peace was upon Him; and with His stripes we are healed."

1 Peter 2:24 – "Who His own self bare our sins in His own body

on the tree, that we, being dead to sins, should live unto righteousness: by whose stripes ye were healed." If I were healed, it means that I am healed. Isaiah was looking to the cross and Peter was looking back at the cross – the redemptive work was done, hallelujah!! Jesus paid the price for our healing! You have to know that healing belongs to you as a child of God!

Some may say, well, I don't know about that healing stuff. My mom and/or grandma were sick and we were praying so hard for their healing. First of all, it's not hard praying that will get results, but praying in faith. Faith is what God honors. Let's look at Isaiah again:

Isaiah 53:4-5 – "Surely He hath borne our griefs, and carried our sorrows: yet we did esteem Him stricken, smitten of God, and afflicted.

Vs 5 – But He was wounded for our transgressions, He was bruised for our iniquities: the chastisement of our peace was upon Him: and with His stripes we are healed."

We are healed now! You have to take your healing! Sickness and disease is not of God. Jesus wants you healed and whole. Faith begins where the will of God is known; the will of God is His word. So throughout the New Testament, we see Jesus going about doing good, and healing all that were "sick and oppressed of the devil."

The redemptive work at calvary has already been done. Jesus has accomplished His earthly mission. Glory to God!

When you find sickness and disease trying to attach itself to your body, you begin to speak to that sickness and disease. Keep the word of God in your eye gate (reading the word) and in your ear gate (hearing CD's or reading the word out aloud.) Jesus is the healer, and healing belongs to you. Begin to thank Him before you even see the manifestation. Jesus wants you well! Sometimes your healing may be instantaneous or it can be gradual. You just have to keep speaking healing scriptures, and <u>believe</u> that you receive your healing when you pray. <u>Luke 17:14b</u> tells us that "<u>as they went, they were cleansed.</u>" This is the account of the ten lepers that Jesus healed!

In my life for about a year, I begin to have symptoms resembling arthritis and the devil began to tell me that, "as you get older, you know that arthritis sometimes will settle in your body, and you just have to live with it." I had an appointment to see my doctor for a regular check up and lo and behold, she said the same thing that the devil told me. She said "you know, arthritis is in that heel and you just have to get you some comfortable shoes to wear." At the time she was telling me this, I was rejecting the words she was speaking. I was saying, "no, I don't have arthritis because with Jesus' stripes I am healed." A side note here: doctors are trained to deal with the symptoms of your health challenge – most are not trained in getting to the root of your health challenge. I have met some wonderful doctors, but my trust is not in the doctor – my trust is in the healer – Jesus Christ. My heel continued to hurt, but as it hurt, I rebuked the pain and would say, "in the Name of Jesus, I take my healing." Today, I am pain free. Take your healing my brother, my sister, because <u>healing belongs to you</u>. It has been bought and paid for by Jesus! Jesus paid a tremendous price for our healing. Command your healing to come to you in Jesus Name!

Sometimes, people may have a tendency to get upset or mad at God for not healing mom or grandma or other family members. Grandma, mom and other family members may have died. Let me say that you don't know what they might have been believing God for. If they were born-again, they may have had a desire to go to be with the Lord. You have to understand that an individual's will comes into play. This is something that we don't have authority over – a human will. God created us as free moral agents. No one has control over your will. Getting back to mom, grandma and family members, you don't know what they were believing God for – they could have given mental assent that they wanted to be healed, but they had a will to go be with the Lord. So just know that if that were the case, no amount of praying could keep them here, but you will see them again one day!

Make this confession over your body everyday: By Jesus stripes, I am healed. I take my healing now! Pain, I command you to leave my body now. Satan, I command you to take your hands off my body in Jesus Name. Jesus, I thank you, and I walk in what has already been given to me. Amen!

CHAPTER 5

ANGELS HAVE BEEN ASSIGNED TO YOU

You need to know that as a born again believer, angels have been assigned to minister for you. Hebrews 1:14 – "Are they not all ministering spirits, sent forth to minister for them who shall be heirs of salvation?" Now I know there are skeptics that say, "I just can't believe that in this day and age in which we live," but if God would open your eyes and allow you to look into the spirit realm, you would see angels. There is a spirit world that is more real than the natural world. My husband often tells of an encounter he had with an angel some years ago. He was in the military stationed at Ft. Eustis, Va. We were in transition from South Carolina to Virginia. We were trying to find a home in Virginia, and had made several trips to Virginia without any success. I had already made my request known to God about specifics I had wanted in my home. So this particular Friday morning, we were traveling back to Virginia for about the fourth time. We stopped in Murfreesboro, North Carolina to get something to eat. He had gone into the restroom to wash his hands when the bathroom door opened and in walked this man. He was of short stature and my husband said he had a "radiance" about him. He simply asked my husband, "how are you doing? Are you doing alright? —everything is going to be alright." After asking those questions, he turned and walked out of the restroom, when the Spirit of God said to my husband, "do you know who you were just talking too? " My husband quickly opened the restroom door, and saw the gentleman disappear! Angels are real. They can take on human form according to Hebrews 13:2 – "Be not forgetful to entertain strangers: for thereby some have entertained angels unawares." Back to our trip: when we got to Newport News, Va., I had a sister that lived there so we stopped by her house, and her phone rang and it was the Realtor that had been working with us. She asked my sister if we were there – this was a puzzle to us also, because we had not told her when we would be up to Virginia again – nor had we told her where we would be. When my husband spoke with the Realtor, she relayed the fact that a house had just been listed, and she would like to meet with us to look at the house. We met with her and went to see the house, and this was exactly what I had asked God for. This was a new house, with neutral carpeting; a certain type counter top in the kitchen; garage and no neighbors behind me – just land. The house had everything I had asked God for including no neighbors behind me with a stream that flowed in the back of the property. I'm talking about angels. In the day and age in which we live, angels are going to become more real to us as we come up against demonic forces.

Psalm 103:20 – "Bless the Lord, ye His angels, that excel in strength, that do His commandments, hearkening unto the voice of His word." As we speak forth the word of Almighty God, we release angels to go forth into battle for us. Release your angels to do your bidding each day. For some of you, I know this sounds a little farfetched, but regardless to how farfetched it may seem, the word of God tells us we have these ministering angels (Hebrews 1:14.) Some of you never give your angels assignments, therefore, they stand around you with nothing to do, so start sending your angels forth in Jesus Name.

Dispatch your angels to go ahead of you to prepare the way before you go out each day – you would be amazed how they divert things that could and should happen to you. They protect you!

Knowing Who You Are In Christ

I am going way back now (this is a throwback as the young people say.) My mother told me years ago, and one of my brothers reminded me of this incident not too long ago. I was just a toddler and my mom had put me in the yard to play. In my early or formative years, life was so simple. Children could go out to play and parents would not have to be concerned about any shootings or kidnappings taking place. We lived on a farm, and I was sitting in the yard playing in the sand. My father had two mules to farm the land – yes, mules. My mother said she looked outside to see what I was doing, and lo and behold, she saw a mule coming my way. The mule was running as hard and as fast as he could- they had broken out of the stalls or stable. Mother said when she saw the mule running my way, she said, "Lord, that mule is heading straight towards my baby." The mule got to me, stopped long enough to look down at me, jumped over me, and started running again. I truly believe my angel stopped that mule. As you think back over your life, you may have encountered angels and didn't even know it.

Psalm 34:7 says – "The angel of the Lord encampeth round about them that fear Him, and delivereth them."

Be very mindful of how you act towards strangers because you could be in the very presence of angels-(Hebrews 13:2.) God has provided everything we need to live a victorious life now!

CHAPTER 6

YOU HAVE BEEN GIVEN AUTHORITY

In the world in which we live today, the children of God have to get hold of the fact that we have authority over the devil. We see in Mark chapter 16 the account of Jesus appearing to His disciples after His resurrection and upbraiding or scolding them for not believing the things that Mary Magdalene told them after she had seen Him. He (Jesus) goes on to give them -after upbraiding them, the commission:

Mark 16:17-20 – "And these signs shall follow them that believe; In my name shall they cast out devils; they shall speak with new tongues;

Vs 18 – They shall take up serpents; and if they drink any deadly thing, it shall not hurt them; they shall lay hands on the sick, and they shall recover.

Vs 19 – So then after the Lord had spoken unto them, He was received up into heaven, and sat on the right hand of God.

Vs. 20 – And They went forth, and preached every where, the Lord working with them, and confirming the word with signs following." If I can take a side journey here: a lot of people like to follow signs and wonders, but no, you follow the Word of God, and signs and wonders will follow the word! We know that the word of God will stand forever.

If you will notice, the first thing Jesus told them in Mark 16:17 was "in His name, they would cast out devils"………..this means that Jesus was giving the believer the authority over demonic spirits. Since that time, the agenda hasn't changed! Jesus still tells us that in His name, we can cast out devils. The New Testament was written for the early church and we are still a part of that Church Age, so whatever was written for the early church applies to the church today. We have authority over demonic forces. Authority means delegated power. Jesus has delegated that authority to us – those that believe in the Lord Jesus Christ and has accepted Him as their Savior.

When did Jesus delegate that authority? Matthew 28:18-20

says, – "And Jesus came and spake unto them, saying, All power is given unto me in heaven and in earth.

Vs 19 – Go ye therefore, and teach all nations, baptizing them in the name of the Father, and of the Son, and of the Holy Ghost:

Vs. 20 – Teaching them to observe all things whatsoever I have commanded you: and, lo, I am with you alway, even unto the end of the world." Amen

We have to realize that Jesus has given us authority: God has given us authority and God Himself is the power behind this authority. This is not my original thought, but it's great just the same. Glory to God!

We see another account of Jesus having sent the seventy out and when they returned, they were excited about the devils being subject to them through His name. Luke 10:18-20 – "And He said unto them, I beheld Satan as lightning fall from heaven. Vs 19 – Behold, I give unto you power to tread on serpents and scorpions, and over all the power of the enemy: and nothing shall by any means hurt you.

Vs 20 – Notwithstanding in this rejoice not, that the spirits are subject unto you; but rather rejoice, because your names are written in heaven."

In Vs 19 - we see Jesus giving power to tread on serpents and scorpions; serpents and scorpions represent demons and evil spirits.

We can look and see how Satan was cast out of heaven in Isaiah 14:12- 15 – "how art thou fallen from heaven, O Lucifer, son of the morning! how art thou cut down to the ground, which didst weaken the nations! Vs 13 – For thou hast said in thine heart, I will ascend into heaven, I will exalt my throne above the stars of God: I will sit also upon the mount of the congregation, in the sides of the north: Vs 14 – I will ascend above the heights of the clouds; I will be like the most High. Vs 15 – Yet thou shalt be brought down to hell, to the sides of the pit."

So we see that Satan exhibited pride in thinking that he would be "like the most High." Even though Satan was in Heaven with God, he wanted to take over. So we know from that time forth, he (Satan) hates mankind – God's greatest creation. He knows where he is going when time is over, and his job is to take as many with him as he can. That's why we have to let people know the good news of the gospel. We have to let them know that hell was not created for man, but for Satan and the angels that fell with him (according to Matthew 25:41.)

I Peter 5:8-9 – "Be sober, be vigilant; because your adversary the devil, as a roaring lion, walketh about, seeking whom he may devour: Vs 9 – Whom resist stedfast in the faith, knowing that the same afflictions are accomplished in your brethren that are in the world."

The word "adversary" means one that is arrayed against you. He walks about "as a roaring loin" seeking whom he may devour. That's why as believers, we have to be vigilant and always remember that we have authority over him (the devil.) You have to establish and settle this in your heart that the greater one lives in you!

<u>1 John 4:4</u> – "Ye are of God, little children, and have overcome them: because greater is He that is in you, than he that is in the world. " You need to say this to yourself often, "the greater one lives in me!" If the greater one lives in you, you have nothing to fear. He has not given us the spirit of fear, but of power, love and a sound mind. I want to build your faith in knowing the authority you have when it comes to the devil. He has no power over you. <u>I John 3:8</u> – "He that committeth sin is of the devil; for the devil sinneth from the beginning. For this purpose the Son of God was manifested, that He might destroy the works of the devil." Jesus destroyed the works of the devil. You see, the devil had mankind trapped with no way out, but when Jesus came, He (Jesus) set the captives free, glory to God! His death, burial and resurrection appeased the Father; thereby giving us access to approach the Father God. Jesus is the mediator between God and man. Thus, we have gained access

back to the Father through Jesus. Therefore, we have to know that no devil in hell can persuade us that he has the greater power. No, Jesus has the greatest power that ever was and ever shall be. Amen! James 2:19 – "Thou believest that there is one God; thou doest well: the devils also believe, and tremble." Many people profess that there is no God – they don't believe that God exists, but even the devil and demons have more sense than that – they know that God exist and they tremble knowing that God does exist and at the end of this age, they will be cast into the bottomless pit – hell forever and ever.

So, it's time for the Army of the living God to arise and take their place. Be bold and let the devil know that "greater is He that is in me, than he that is in the world."

Ephesians 1:19-22 – "And what is the exceeding greatness of His power to us-ward who believe, according to the working of His mighty power, Vs. 20 – Which He wrought in Christ, when He raised Him from the dead, and set Him at his own right hand in the heavenly places, Vs 21 – Far above all principality, and power, and might, and dominion, and every name that is named, not only in this world, but also in that which is to come: Vs. 22 – And hath put all things under His feet, and gave Him to be the head over all things to the church." You have to know that you have authority over the devil and nothing shall by any means hurt you!

CHAPTER 7

HOLINESS IS STILL REQUIRED

I Peter 1:15-16 – "But as He which hath called you is holy, so be ye holy in all manner of conversation;

Vs. 16 – Because it is written, Be ye holy; for I am holy."

Knowing who you are in Christ let's you know that God is holy and He commands us to be holy. In certain denominational circles, they take Holiness to be: the way you dress and look– no make-up; long dresses etc. – to them, holiness is more of an outward show, rather than accepting the redemptive work that Christ did on calvary for all mankind.

1 Timothy 2:9-10 says, - "In like manner also, that women adorn

themselves in modest apparel, with shamefacedness and sobriety; not with broided hair, or gold, or pearls, or costly array;

Vs. 10 – But (which becometh women professing godliness) with good works." <u>Modest apparel</u> - what does that mean? One definition is: behaving according to standard of what is proper or decorous; decent; pure; not displaying one's body.

Now the Amplified makes this scripture clearer. Here is what the same scripture says: <u>I Timothy 2:9 -10</u>– "Also (I desire) that women should adorn themselves modestly and appropriately and sensibly in seemly apparel, not with (elaborate) hair arrangement or gold or pearls or expensive clothing,

Vs. 10 – But by doing good deeds – that is, deeds in themselves good, and for the good and advantage of those contacted by them – as befits women who profess reverential fear for and devotion to God."

Women of God, this scripture tells us that we should be showing women of the world what it looks like to be properly dressed and poised to maintain a Godly testimony. Before you leave the house each day, take a moment to look in the mirror and just ask the simple question, "would God be pleased with me today?" Is my blouse too revealing or is my skirt too tight? Just who am I trying to tempt or attract? If you are looking to attract a man – you shouldn't be doing the looking, for the bible says in Proverbs 18:22 – "Whoso findeth a wife findeth a good thing, and obtaineth favour of the Lord." So this lets us know that the man is suppose to be doing the pursuing. He should be pursuing you, woman of God, not the other way around. So ladies, if you chase after God, then the man will pursue you.

Holiness to the Lord! Holiness in the times in which we live seems to be such an antiquated word, but you have to understand that God does not change – He still requires us to be holy. Hebrews 13:8 says - "Jesus Christ the same yesterday, and today, and for ever." His command for holiness hasn't changed. Hebrews 12:14 – "Follow peace with all men, and holiness, without which no man shall see the Lord:"

Holiness means that I'm in agreement with God's word and I obey His word. Remember, when you name the name of Jesus, people are watching you. What are they seeing? My husband says, "it's a good thing if you are doing the right thing." The part of scripture that says, "without holiness, no man shall see the Lord…." we need to ask ourselves this question; just what is this scripture saying? This means that when you don't line up with the word of God, the world doesn't get a real view of who Jesus is. Our desire everyday should be to be more like Jesus. We are to be imitators of Jesus! How was Jesus? He was the epitomy of love! He loved so much until He died so that you and I could have a right to the tree of life; we should be people of love. He was full of compassion, therefore, we should be people of compassion. He had so much compassion for the people in His day until He was willing to die in order to set the captives free; He opened blinded eyes and every where He went, He had a following because the people knew that He truly loved and cared for them – so it is today. People don't really care how much you know, but they want to know that you care for them. Jesus loves us so much and He cares so much about us until we ought to be able to tell the good news of the gospel everywhere we go. Jesus – yes Jesus, loves us and He thoroughly looks for us to live a holy, pure and consecrated life –we let our light shine so that men can see our good works and glorify our Father which is in heaven.

<u>Colossians 1:22</u> – "In the body of His flesh through death, to present you holy and unblameable and unreproveable in His sight:" Jesus paid a tremendous price for us to be holy, unblameable and unreproveable in His sight – what an awesome God we serve. Therefore, knowing who you are in Christ will give you the assurance that you are holy unto the Lord and you will know that you have been set apart for God. We are going from glory to glory!

We as the body of Christ have a 'high calling.' We ought to enter the house of God in a state of <u>awe</u> and <u>respect</u> because

He is in His holy temple and we as His body ought to enter with reverence and respect. I'm sure if we were invited to visit the President or another dignitary, we would want to be dressed for the occasion, yet some come to the house of God, with no regard to the fact that we are coming to meet the King. He is the King of Kings and the Lord of Lords!

If we were invited to visit the President, a lot of us would buy an outfit on our charge cards, etc. just to dress the part. "We would dress to impress." How much more important is our King – Jesus! Let us enter into His gates with thanksgiving and into His courts with praise – looking good for Jesus! We know that God looks at the heart, not at the outward appearance, but let's make our heavenly Father truly aware of how much we appreciate Him by honoring Him with the way we are dressed. We are going to the house of the Lord, not to the beach or a ball game. We are to honor our King!

We don't have to go out and buy a new wardrobe to come to the house of God, but we should be willing to be led by the Spirit of God on what would be pleasing to the Lord. We should want to please God in every area of our life.

Holiness is right, because this is what the Lord requires of His children, and today we hear very little about holiness. It is not a very popular subject because it may remind us as stated earlier of the long dresses; no make-up, etc., and the appearance of trying to <u>look holy</u> instead of <u>being holy</u>. I can recall in my own life before I came to the Lord, I saw a lady with the long dress and the cotton stockings and I can remember thinking: if I have to look that way to be born again, I will never be born again. Thank God I later learned better. Remember that Holiness is being in agreement with God. Whatever is written in God's word, you choose to agree with and obey it. You love the Lord and want to please Him in every area of your life.

So regardless to how fast paced the world we live in becomes, holiness is still required.

CHAPTER 8

WE HAVE THE ASSURANCE THAT HEAVEN WILL BE OUR FINAL AND ETERNAL DESTINATION

We shall finally see Jesus face to face!

<u>Revelation 22:1-4</u> – "And he shewed me a pure river of water of life, clear as crystal, proceeding out of the throne of God and of the Lamb.

Vs. 2 – In the midst of the street of it, and on either side of the river, was there the tree of life, which bare twelve manner of fruits, and yielded her fruit every month: and the leaves of the tree were for the healing of the nations.

Vs. 3 – And there shall be no more curse: but the throne of God and of the Lamb shall be in it; and His servants shall serve Him:

Vs. 4 – And they shall see His face; and His name shall be in their foreheads."

We will never have any more disappointments; no more heartaches; and no more tears for God shall wipe away all tears from our eyes. We will be with our Lord and Savior, Jesus Christ forever and all eternity. Can you just imagine what that will be like? Just think about that for a moment!

A few months ago, I talked to a very dear sister in the Lord, and she alluded to the fact that she felt like she was not good enough to be used by God. I assured her that she is in the exact place that the devil wants her to be. I reminded her that it's not through our own righteousness that we are good enough, but by the precious blood of Jesus that we are made righteous. Ephesians 2:8-9 – "For by grace are ye saved through faith; and that not of yourselves: it is the gift of God:

Vs. 9 – Not of works, lest any man should boast."

Heaven is on our agenda! We can be assured of the fact that soon and very soon, we are going to see the King! Don't let Satan deter you from fulfilling the call and purpose God has for your life. Our ultimate goal is being in heaven with Jesus. As the body of Christ, we should make up in our mind that whatever it takes in this life to get there, we will obey God's written word and live accordingly.

Revelation 21:1-7 – "And I saw a new heaven and a new earth: for the first heaven and the first earth were passed away; and there was no more sea.

Vs. 2 – And I John saw the holy city, new Jerusalem, coming down from God out of heaven, prepared as a bride adorned for her husband.

Vs. 3 – And I heard a great voice out of heaven saying, Behold, the tabernacle of God is with men, and He will dwell with them, and they shall be His people, and God Himself shall be with them, and be their God.

Vs. 4 – And God shall wipe away all tears from their eyes; and there shall be no more death, neither sorrow, nor crying, neither shall there be any more pain: for the former things are passed away.

Vs. 5 – And He that sat upon the throne said, Behold, I make all things new. And He said unto me, Write: for these words are true and faithful.

Vs. 6 – And He said unto me, It is done. I am Alpha and Omega, the beginning and the end. I will give unto him that is athirst of the fountain of the water of life freely.

Knowing Who You Are In Christ

Vs. 7 – He that overcometh shall inherit all things; and I will be his God, and he shall be my son."

What an awesome promise from God! We shall see Him as He really is! Glory to God!! Just one glimpse of heaven will pay for all and everything we have had to go through in this life.

<u>Revelation 22:12-13</u> – "And, behold, I come quickly; and my reward is with me, to give every man according as his work shall be.

Vs. 13 – I am Alpha and Omega, the beginning and the end, the first and the last."

Just remember that because of who you are in Christ, He has made everything available to you, and all you have to do is totally commit and submit your life to Him.

When knowing who you are in Christ becomes a reality in your life, you will do great exploits for the Kingdom of God!

CONCLUSION

In this final hour of the church – the body of Christ, let us rise up and take our place. Our prayer should be that "the eyes of our understanding would be enlightened; that we may know what is the hope of His calling, and what the riches of the glory of His inheritance in the saints" – (Ephesians 1:18.) We need to know that the Lord says that we are more than conquerors – not just conquerors! Romans 8:37 says, – "Nay, in all these things we are more than conquerors through Him that loved us." We have been given authority! When He left the earth to go back to His heavenly home, He delegated that authority to us. Let us begin to walk in all that has been provided for us. Take your rightful place and "Know Who You Are In Christ!!" You are valuable and precious in God's sight.

Stay blessed!

Made in the USA
Columbia, SC
29 July 2022